The Initiation of the Pyramid

Manly Palmer Hall

Revised and Edited by
Dennis Logan

[2020]

Copyright 2020 by Rolled Scroll Publishing

ISBN: 9781952900143

The Initiation of the Pyramid

SUPREME among the wonders of antiquity, unrivaled by the achievements of later architects and builders, the Great Pyramid of Gizeh bears mute witness to an unknown civilization which, having completed its predestined span, passed into oblivion. Eloquent in its silence, inspiring in its majesty, divine in its simplicity, the Great Pyramid is indeed a sermon in stone. Its magnitude overwhelms the puny sensibilities of man. Among the shifting sands of time it stands as a fitting emblem of eternity itself. Who were the illumined mathematicians who planned its parts and dimensions, the master craftsmen who supervised its construction, the skilled artisans who trued its blocks of stone?

The earliest and best-known account of the building of the Great Pyramid is that given by that highly revered but somewhat imaginative historian, Herodotus. "The pyramid was built in steps, battlement-wise, as it is called, or, according to others, altar-wise. After laying the stones for the base, they raised the remaining stones to their places by means of machines formed of short wooden planks. The first machine raised them from the ground to the top of the first step. On this there was another machine, which received the stone upon its arrival, and conveyed it to the second step, whence a third machine advanced it still higher. Either they had as many machines as there were steps in the pyramid, or possibly they had but a single machine, which, being easily moved, was transferred from tier to tier as the stone rose. Both accounts are given, and therefore I mention both. The upper portion of the pyramid was finished first, then the middle, and finally the part which was lowest and nearest the ground. There is an inscription in Egyptian characters on the pyramid which records the quantity of radishes, onions, and garlick consumed by the labourers who constructed it; and I perfectly well remember that the interpreter who read the writing to me said that the money expended in this way was 1600 talents of silver. If this then is a true record, what a vast sum must have been spent on the iron tools used in the work, and on the feeding and clothing of the labourers, considering the length of time the work lasted, which has already been stated [ten years], and the additional time--no small space, I imagine--which must have been occupied by the quarrying of the stones, their conveyance, and the formation of the underground apartments."

While his account is extremely colorful, it is apparent that the Father of History, for reasons which he doubtless considered sufficient, concocted a fraudulent story to conceal the true origin and purpose of the Great Pyramid. This is but one of several instances in his writings which would lead the thoughtful reader to suspect that Herodotus himself was an initiate of the Sacred Schools and consequently obligated to preserve inviolate the secrets of the ancient orders. The theory advanced by Herodotus and now generally accepted that the Pyramid was the tomb of the Pharaoh Cheops cannot be substantiated. In fact, Manetho, Eratosthenes, and Diodorus Siculus all differ from Herodotus--as well as from each other--regarding the name of the builder of this supreme edifice. The sepulchral vault, which, according to the Lepsius Law of pyramid construction, should have been finished at the same time as the monument or sooner, was never completed. There is no proof that the building was erected by the Egyptians, for the elaborate carvings with which the burial chambers of Egyptian royalty are almost invariably ornamented are entirely lacking and it embodies none of the elements of their architecture or decoration, such as inscriptions, images, cartouches, paintings, and other distinctive features associated with dynastic mortuary art. The only hieroglyphics to be found within the Pyramid are a few builders' marks sealed up in the *chambers of construction*, first opened by Howard Vyse. These apparently were painted upon the stones before they were set in position, for in a number of instances the marks were either inverted or disfigured by the operation of fitting the blocks together. While Egyptologists have attempted to identify the crude dabs of paint as cartouches of Cheops, it is almost inconceivable that this ambitious ruler would have permitted his royal name to suffer such indignities. As the most eminent authorities on the subject are still uncertain as to the true meaning of these crude markings, whatever proof they might be that the building was erected during the fourth dynasty is certainly offset by the sea shells at the base of the Pyramid which Mr. Gab advances as evidence that it was erected before the Deluge--a theory substantiated by the much-abused Arabian traditions. One Arabian historian declared that the Pyramid was built by the Egyptian sages as a refuge against the Flood, while another proclaimed it to have been the treasure house of the powerful antediluvian king Sheddad Ben Ad. A panel of hieroglyphs over the entrance, which the casual observer might consider to afford a solution of the mystery, unfortunately dates back no further than A.D. 1843, having been cut at that time by Dr. Lepsius as a tribute to the King of Prussia.

Caliph al Mamoun, an illustrious descendant of the Prophet, inspired by stories of the immense treasures sealed within its depths, journeyed from Bagdad to Cairo, A.D. 820, with a great force of workmen to open the mighty Pyramid. When Caliph al Mamoun first reached the foot of the "Rock of Ages" and gazed up at its smooth glistening surface, a tumult of emotions undoubtedly racked his soul. The casing stones must have been in place at the time of his visit, for the Caliph could find no indication of an entrance--four perfectly smooth surfaces confronted him. Following vague rumors, he set his followers to work on the north side of the Pyramid, with instructions to keep on cutting and chiseling until they discovered something. To the Moslems with their crude instruments and vinegar it was a herculean effort to tunnel a full hundred feet through the limestone. Many times they were on the point of rebellion, but the word of the Caliph was law and the hope of a vast fortune buoyed them up.

At last on the eve of total discouragement fate came to their rescue. A great stone was heard to fall somewhere in the wall near the toiling and disgruntled Arabs. Pushing on toward the sound with renewed enthusiasm, they finally broke into the descending passage which leads into the subterranean chamber. They then chiseled their way around the great stone portcullis which had fallen into a position barring their progress, and attacked and removed one after another the granite plugs which for a while continued to slide down the passage leading from the Queen's Chamber above.

Finally no more blocks descended and the way was clear for the followers of the Prophet. But where were the treasures? From room to room the frantic workmen rushed, looking in vain for loot. The discontent of the Moslems reached such a height that Caliph al Mamoun--who had inherited much of the wisdom of his illustrious father, the Caliph al Raschid--sent to Bagdad for funds, which he caused to be secretly buried near the entrance of the Pyramid. He then ordered his men to dig at that spot and great was their rejoicing when the treasure was discovered, the workmen being deeply impressed by the wisdom of the antediluvian monarch who had carefully estimated their wages and thoughtfully caused the exact amount to be buried for their benefit!

The Caliph then returned to the city of his fathers and the Great Pyramid was left to the mercy of succeeding generations. In the ninth century the sun's rays striking the highly polished surfaces of the original casing stones caused each side of the Pyramid to appear as a dazzling triangle of light. Since that time, all but two of these casing stones have disappeared. Investigation has resulted in their discovery, recut and resurfaced, in the walls of Mohammedan mosques and palaces in various parts of Cairo and its environs.

ŒDIPUS AND THE SPHINX.

From Levi's *Les Mystères de la Kaballe*.

The Egyptian Sphinx is closely related to the Greek legend of Œdipus, who first solved the famous riddle propounded by the mysterious creature with the body of a winged lion and the head of a woman which frequented the highway leading to Thebes. To each who passed her lair the sphinx addressed the question, "What animal is it that in the morning goes on four feet, at noon on two feet, and in the evening on three feet?" These who failed to answer her riddle she destroyed. Œdipus declared the answer to be man himself, who in childhood crawled upon his hands and knees, in manhood stood erect, and in old age shuffled along supporting himself by a staff. Discovering one who knew the answer to her riddle, the sphinx cast herself from the cliff which bordered the road and perished.

There is still another answer to the riddle of the sphinx, an answer best revealed by a consideration of the Pythagorean values of numbers. The 4, the 2 and the 3 produce the sum of 9, which is the natural number of man and also of the lower worlds. The 4 represents the ignorant man, the 2 the intellectual man, and the 3 the spiritual man. Infant humanity walks on four legs, evolving humanity on two legs, and to the power of his own mind the redeemed and illumined magus adds the staff of wisdom. The sphinx is therefore the mystery of Nature, the embodiment of the secret doctrine, and all who cannot solve her riddle perish. To pass the sphinx is to attain personal immortality.

PYRAMID PROBLEMS

C. Piazzi Smyth asks: "Was the Great Pyramid, then, erected before the invention of hieroglyphics, and previous to the birth of the

Egyptian religion?" Time may yet prove that the upper chambers of the Pyramid were a sealed mystery before the establishment of the Egyptian empire. In the subterranean chamber, however, are markings which indicate that the Romans gained admission there. In the light of the secret philosophy of the Egyptian initiates, W. W. Harmon, by a series of extremely complicated yet exact mathematical calculations; determines that the first ceremonial of the Pyramid was performed 68,890 years ago on the occasion when the star Vega for the first time sent its ray down the descending passage into the pit. The actual building of the Pyramid was accomplished in the period of from ten to fifteen years immediately preceding this date.

While such figures doubtless will evoke the ridicule of modern Egyptologists, they are based upon an exhaustive study of the principles of sidereal mechanics as incorporated into the structure of the Pyramid by its initiated builders. If the casing stones were in position at the beginning of the ninth century, the so-called erosion marks upon the outside were not due to water. The theory also that the salt upon the interior stones of the Pyramid is evidence that the building was once submerged is weakened by the scientific fact that this kind of stone is subject to exudations of salt. While the building may have been submerged, at least in part, during the many thousands of years since its erection, the evidence adduced to prove this point is not conclusive.

The Great Pyramid was built of limestone and granite throughout, the two kinds of rock being combined in a peculiar and significant manner. The stones were trued with the utmost precision, and the cement used was of such remarkable quality that it is now practically as hard as the stone itself. The limestone blocks were sawed with bronze saws, the teeth of which were diamonds or other jewels. The chips from the stones were piled against the north side of the plateau on which the structure stands, where they form an additional buttress to aid in supporting the weight of the structure. The entire Pyramid is an example of perfect orientation and actually squares the circle. This last is accomplished by dropping a vertical line from the apex of the Pyramid to its base line. If this vertical line be considered as the radius of an imaginary circle, the length of the circumference of such a circle will be found to equal the sum of the base lines of the four sides of the Pyramid.

If the passage leading to the King's Chamber and the Queen's Chamber was sealed up thousands of years before the Christian Era, those later admitted into the Pyramid Mysteries must have received their initiations in subterranean galleries now unknown. Without such galleries there could have been no possible means of ingress or egress, since the single surface entrance was completely dosed with casing stones. If not blocked by the mass of the Sphinx or concealed in some part of that image, the secret entrance may be either in one of the adjacent temples or upon the sides of the limestone plateau.

Attention is called to the granite plugs filling the ascending passageway to the Queen's Chamber which Caliph al Mamoun was forced practically to pulverize before he could clear a way into the upper chambers. C. Piazzi Smyth notes that the positions of the stones demonstrate that they were set in place from above--which made it necessary for a considerable number of workmen to depart from the upper chambers. How did they do it? Smyth believes they descended through the well (see diagram), dropping the ramp stone into place behind them. He further contends that robbers probably used the well as a means of getting into the upper chambers. The ramp stone having been set in a bed of plaster, the robbers were forced to break through it, leaving a jagged opening. Mr. Dupré, an architect who has spent years investigating the pyramids, differs from Smyth, however, in that he believes the well itself to be a robbers' hole, being the first successful attempt made to enter the upper chambers from the subterranean chamber, then the only open section of the Pyramid.

Mr. Dupré bases his conclusion upon the fact that the well is merely a rough hole and the grotto an irregular chamber, without any evidence of the architectural precision with which the remainder of the structure was erected. The diameter of the well also precludes the possibility of its having been dug downward; it must have been gouged out from below, and the grotto was necessary to supply air to the thieves. It is inconceivable that the Pyramid builders would break one of their own ramp stones and leave its broken surface and a gaping hole in the side wall of their otherwise perfect gallery. If the well is a robbers' hole, it may explain why the Pyramid was empty when Caliph al Mamoun entered it and what happened to the missing coffer lid. A careful examination of the so-called unfinished subterranean chamber, which must have been the base of operations for the robbers, might disclose traces of their presence or show where they piled the rubble which must have accumulated as a result of their operations. While it is not entirely clear by what entrance the robbers reached the subterranean chamber, it is improbable that they used the descending passageway.

There is a remarkable niche in the north wall of the Queen's Chamber which the Mohammedan guides glibly pronounce to be a shrine. The general shape of this niche, however, with its walls converging by a series of overlaps like those of the Grand Gallery, would indicate that originally it had been intended as a passageway. Efforts made to explore this niche have been nonproductive, but Mr. Dupré believes an entrance to exist here through which--if the well did not exist at the time--the workmen made their exit from the Pyramid after dropping the stone plugs into the ascending gallery.

Biblical scholars have contributed a number of most extraordinary conceptions regarding the Great Pyramid. This ancient edifice has been identified by them as Joseph's granary (despite its hopelessly inadequate capacity); as the tomb prepared for the unfortunate Pharaoh of the Exodus who could not be buried there because his body was never recovered from the Red Sea; and finally as a perpetual confirmation of the infallibility of the numerous prophecies contained in the Authorized Version!

THE SPHINX

Although the Great Pyramid, as Ignatius Donnelly has demonstrated, is patterned after an antediluvian type of architecture, examples of which are to be found in nearly every part of the world, the Sphinx

(*Hu*) is typically Egyptian. The stele between its paws states the Sphinx is an image of the Sun God, Harmackis, which was evidently made in the similitude of the Pharaoh during whose reign it was chiseled. The statue was restored and completely excavated by Tahutmes IV as the result of a vision in which the god had appeared and declared himself oppressed by the weight of the sand about his body. The broken beard of the Sphinx was discovered during excavations between the front paws. The steps leading up to the sphinx and also the temple and altar between the paws are much later additions, probably Roman, for it is known that the Romans reconstructed many Egyptian antiquities. The shallow depression in the crown of the head, once thought to be the terminus of a closed up passageway leading from the Sphinx to the Great Pyramid, was merely intended to help support a headdress now missing.

Metal rods have been driven into the Sphinx in a vain effort to discover chambers or passages within its body. The major part of the Sphinx is a single stone, but the front paws have been built up of smaller stones. The Sphinx is about 200 feet long, 70 feet high, and 38 feet wide across the shoulders. The main stone from which it was carved is believed by some to have been transported from distant quarries by methods unknown, while others assert it to be native rock, possibly an outcropping somewhat resembling the form into which it was later carved. The theory once advanced that both the Pyramid and the Sphinx were built from artificial stones made on the spot has been abandoned. A careful analysis of the limestone shows it to be composed of small sea creatures called *mummulites*.

The popular supposition that the Sphinx was the true portal of the Great Pyramid, while it survives with surprising tenacity, has never been substantiated. P. Christian presents this theory as follows, basing it in part upon the authority of Iamblichus:

*****"The Sphinx of Gizeh, says the author of the Traité des Mystères, served as the entrance to the sacred subterranean chambers in which the trials of the initiate were undergone. This entrance, obstructed in our day by sands and rubbish, may still be traced between the forelegs of the crouched colossus. It was formerly closed by a bronze gate whose secret spring could be operated only by the Magi. It was guarded by public respect: and a sort of religious fear maintained its inviolability better than armed protection would have done. In the belly of the Sphinx were cut out galleries leading to the subterranean part of the Great Pyramid. These galleries were so artfully crisscrossed along their course to the Pyramid that in setting forth into the passage without a guide through this network, one ceaselessly and inevitably returned to the starting point." (See *Histoire de la Magie*.)

Unfortunately, the bronze door referred to cannot be found, nor is there any evidence that it ever existed. The passing centuries have wrought many changes in the colossus, however, and the original opening may have been closed.

Nearly all students of the subject believe that subterranean chambers exist beneath the Great Pyramid. Robert Ballard writes: "The priests of the Pyramids of Lake Mœris had their vast subterranean residences. It appears to me more than probable that those of Gizeh were similarly provided. And I may go further:--Out of these very caverns may have been excavated the limestone of which the Pyramids were built. * * * In the bowels of the limestone ridge on which the Pyramids are built will yet be found, I feel convinced, ample information as to their uses. A good diamond drill with two or three hundred feet of rods is what is wanted to test this, and the solidarity of the Pyramids at the same time." (See *The Solution of the Pyramid Problem.*)

Mr. Ballard's theory of extensive underground apartments and quarries brings up an important problem in architectonics. The Pyramid builders were too farsighted to endanger the permanence of the Great Pyramid by placing over five million tons of limestone and granite on any but a solid foundation. It is therefore reasonably certain that such chambers or passageways as may exist beneath the building are relatively insignificant, like those within the body of the structure, which occupy less than one sixteen-hundredth of the cubic contents of the Pyramid.

The Sphinx was undoubtedly erected for symbolical purposes at the instigation of the priestcraft. The theories that the uræus upon its forehead was originally the finger of an immense sundial and that both the Pyramid and the Sphinx were used to measure time, the seasons, and the precession of the equinoxes are ingenious but not wholly convincing. If this great creature was erected to obliterate the ancient passageway leading into the subterranean temple of the Pyramid, its symbolism would be most appropriate. In comparison with the overwhelming size and dignity of the Great Pyramid, the Sphinx is almost insignificant. Its battered face, upon which may still be seen vestiges of the red paint with which the figure was originally covered, is disfigured beyond recognition. Its nose was broken off by a fanatical Mohammedan, lest the followers of the Prophet be led into idolatry. The very nature of its construction and the present repairs necessary to prevent the head from falling off indicate that it could not have survived the great periods of time which have elapsed since the erection of the Pyramid.

To the Egyptians, the Sphinx was the symbol of strength and intelligence. It was portrayed as androgynous to signify that they recognized the initiates and gods as partaking of both the positive and negative creative powers. Gerald Massey writes: "This is the secret of the Sphinx. The orthodox sphinx of Egypt is masculine in front and feminine behind. So is the image of Sut-Typhon, a type of horn and tail, male in front and female behind. The Pharaohs, who wore the tail of the Lioness or Cow behind them, were male in front and female behind. Like the Gods they included the dual totality of Being in one person, born of the Mother, but of both sexes as the Child." (See *The Natural Genesis*.)

Most investigators have ridiculed the Sphinx and, without even deigning to investigate the great colossus, have turned their attention to the more overwhelming mystery of the Pyramid.

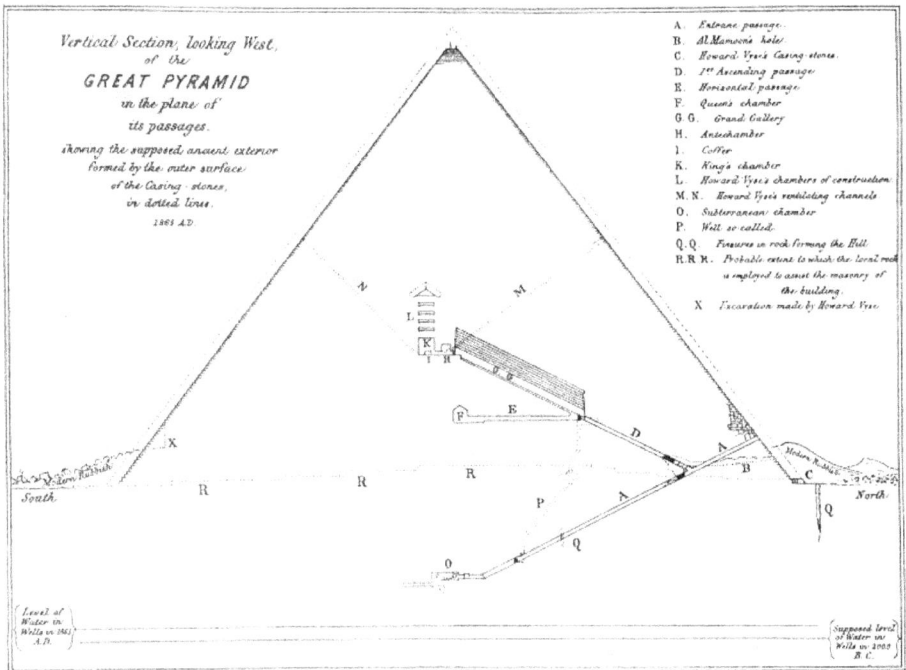

A VERTICAL SECTION OF THE GREAT PYRAMID.

From Smyth's *Life and Wok at the Great Pyramid.*

The Great Pyramid stands upon a limestone plateau at the base of which, according to ancient history, the Nile once flooded, thus supplying a method for the huge blocks used in its construction. Presuming that the capstone as originally in place, the Pyramid is, according to John Taylor, in round figures 486 feet high; the base of each side is 764 feet long, and the entire structure covers a ground area of more than 13 acres.

The Great Pyramid is the only one in the group at Gizeh--in fact, as far as known, the only one in Egypt--that has chambers within the actual body of the Pyramid itself. Far this reason it is said to refute the Lepsius Law, which asserts that each of these structures is a monument raised over a subterranean chamber in which a ruler is entombed. The Pyramid contains four chambers, which in the diagram are lettered K, H, F, and O.

The King's Chamber (K) is an oblong apartment 39 feet long, 17 felt wide, and 19 feet high (disregarding fractional parts of a foot in each case), with a flat roof consisting of nine great stones, the largest in the Pyramid. Above the King's Chamber are five low compartments (L), generally termed construction chambers. In the lowest of these the so-called hieroglyphs of the Pharaoh

Cheops are located. The roof of the fifth construction chamber is peaked. At the end of the King's Chamber opposite the entrance stands the famous sarcophagus, or coffer (I), and behind it is a shallow opening that was dug in the hope of discovering valuables. Two air vents (M, N) passing through the entire body of the Pyramid ventilate the King's Chamber. In itself this is sufficient to establish that the building was not intended for a tomb.

Between the upper end of the Grand Gallery (G. G.) and the King's Chamber is a small antechamber (H), its extreme length 9 feet, its extreme width 5 feet, and its extreme height 12 feet, with its walls grooved far purposes now unknown. In the groove nearest the Grand Gallery is a slab of stone in two sections, with a peculiar boss or knob protruding about an inch from the surface of the upper part facing the Grand Gallery. This stone does not reach to the floor of the antechamber and those entering the King's Chamber must pass under the slab. From the King's Chamber, the Grand Gallery--157 feet in length, 28 feet in height, 7 feet in width at its widest point and decreasing to 3½ feet as the result of seven converging overlaps, of the stones forming the walls--descends to a little above the level of the Queen's Chamber. Here a gallery (E) branches off, passing mere than 100 feet back towards the center of the Pyramid and opening into the Queen's Chamber (F). The Queen's Chamber is 19 feet long, 17 feet wide, and 20 feet high. Its roof is peaked and composed of great slabs of stone. Air passages not shown lead from the Queen's Chamber, but these were not open originally. In the east wall of the Queen's Chamber is a peculiar niche of gradually converging stone, which in all likelihood, may prove to be a new lost entrance way.

At the paint where the Grand Gallery ends and the horizontal passage towards the Queen's Chamber begins is the entrance to the well and also the opening leading down the first ascending passage (D) to the point where this passage meets the descending passage (A) leading from the outer wall of the Pyramid down to the subterranean chamber. After descending 59 feet down the well (P), the grotto is reached. Continuing through the floor of the grotto the well leads downward 133 feet to the descending entrance passage (A), which it meets a short distance before this passage becomes horizontal and leads into the subterranean chamber.

The subterranean chamber (O) is about 46 feet long and 27 feet wide, but is extremely low, the ceiling varying in height from a little over 3 feet to about 13 feet from the rough and apparently unfinished floor. From the south side of the subterranean chamber a low tunnel runs about 50 feet and then meets a blank wall. These constitute the only known openings in the Pyramid, with the exception of a few niches, exploration holes, blind passages, and the rambling cavernous tunnel (B) hewn out by the Moslems under the leadership of the Prophet's descendant, Caliph al Mamoun.

THE PYRAMID MYSTERIES

The word pyramid is popularly supposed to be derived from πῦρ, fire, thus signifying that it is the symbolic representation of the One Divine Flame, the life of every creature. John Taylor believes the word pyramid to mean a "measure of wheat, " while C. Piazzi Smyth favors the Coptic meaning, "a division into ten." The initiates of old accepted the pyramid form as the ideal symbol of both the secret doctrine and those institutions established for its dissemination. Both pyramids and mounds are antitypes of the Holy Mountain, or High Place of God, which was believed to stand in the "midst" of the earth. John P. Lundy relates the Great Pyramid to the fabled Olympus, further assuming that its subterranean passages correspond to the tortuous byways of Hades.

The square base of the Pyramid is a constant reminder that the House of Wisdom is firmly founded upon Nature and her immutable laws. "The Gnostics," writes Albert Pike, "claimed that the whole edifice of their science rested on a square whose angles were: Σιγη, Silence; Βυθος, Profundity; Νους, Intelligence; and Αληθεια Truth." (See *Morals and Dogma*.) The sides of the Great Pyramid face the four cardinal angles, the latter signifying according to Eliphas Levi the extremities of heat and cold (south and north) and the extremities of light and darkness (east and west). The base of the Pyramid further represents the four material elements or substances from the combinations of which the quaternary body of man is formed. From each side of the square there rises a triangle, typifying the threefold divine being enthroned within every quaternary material nature. If each base line be considered a square from which ascends a threefold spiritual power, then the sum of the lines of the four faces (12) and the four hypothetical squares (16) constituting the base is 28, the sacred number of the lower world. If this be added to the three septenaries composing the sun (21), it equals 49, the square of 7 and the number of the universe.

The twelve signs of the zodiac, like the Governors' of the lower worlds, are symbolized by the twelve lines of the four triangles--the faces of the Pyramid. In the midst of each face is one of the beasts of Ezekiel, and the structure as a whole becomes the Cherubim. The three main chambers of the Pyramid are related to the heart, the brain, and the generative system--the spiritual centers of the human constitution. The triangular form of the Pyramid also is similar to the posture assumed by the body during the ancient meditative exercises. The Mysteries taught that the divine energies from the gods descended upon the top of the Pyramid, which was likened to an inverted tree with its branches below and its roots at the apex. From this inverted tree the divine wisdom is disseminated by streaming down the diverging sides and radiating throughout the world.

The size of the capstone of the Great Pyramid cannot be accurately determined, for, while most investigators have assumed that it was once in place, no vestige of it now remains. There is a curious tendency among the builders of great religious edifices to leave their creations unfinished, thereby signifying that God alone is complete. The capstone--if it existed--was itself a miniature pyramid, the apex of which again would be capped by a smaller block of similar shape, and so on *ad infinitum*. The capstone therefore is the epitome of the entire structure. Thus, the Pyramid may be likened to the universe and the capstone to man. Following the chain of analogy, the mind is the capstone of man, the spirit the capstone of the mind, and God--the epitome of the whole--the capstone of the spirit. As a rough and unfinished block, man is taken from the quarry and by the secret culture of the Mysteries gradually transformed into a trued and perfect pyramidal capstone. The temple is complete only when the initiate himself becomes the living apex through which the divine power is focused into the diverging structure below.

W. Marsham Adams calls the Great Pyramid "the House of the Hidden Places"; such indeed it was, for it represented the inner sanctuary of pre-Egyptian wisdom. By the Egyptians the Great Pyramid was associated with Hermes, the god of wisdom and letters and the Divine Illuminator worshiped through the planet Mercury. Relating Hermes to the Pyramid emphasizes anew the fact that it was in reality the supreme temple of the Invisible and Supreme Deity. The Great Pyramid was not a lighthouse, an observatory, or a tomb, but the first temple of the Mysteries, the first structure erected as a repository for those secret truths which are the certain foundation of all arts and sciences. It was the perfect emblem of the *microcosm* and the *macrocosm* and, according to the secret teachings, the tomb of Osiris, the black god of the Nile. Osiris represents a certain manifestation of solar energy, and therefore his house or tomb is emblematic of the universe within which he is entombed and upon the cross of which he is crucified.

Through the mystic passageways and chambers of the Great Pyramid passed the illumined of antiquity. They entered its portals as *men*; they came forth as *gods*. It was the place of the "second birth," the "womb of the Mysteries," and wisdom dwelt in it as God dwells in the hearts of men. Somewhere in the depths of its recesses there resided an unknown being who was called "The Initiator," or "The Illustrious One," robed in blue and gold and bearing in his hand the sevenfold key of Eternity. This was the lion-faced hierophant, the Holy One, the Master of Masters, who never left the House of Wisdom and whom no man ever saw save he who had passed through the gates of preparation and purification. It was in these chambers that Plato--he of the broad brow---came face to face with the wisdom of the ages personified in the Master of the Hidden House.

Who was the Master dwelling in the mighty Pyramid, the many rooms of which signified the worlds in space; the Master whom none might behold save those who had been "born again"? He alone fully knew the secret of the Pyramid, but he has departed the way of the wise and the house is empty. The hymns of praise no longer echo in muffled tones through the chambers; the neophyte no longer passes through the elements and wanders among the seven stars; the candidate no longer receives the "Word of Life" from the lips of the Eternal One. Nothing now remains that the eye of man can see but an empty shell--the outer symbol of an inner truth--and men call the House of God a tomb!

The technique of the Mysteries was unfolded by the Sage Illuminator, the Master of the Secret House. The power to know his guardian spirit was revealed to the new initiate; the method of disentangling his material body from. his divine vehicle was explained; and to consummate the *magnum opus*, there was revealed the Divine Name-- the secret and unutterable designation of the Supreme Deity, by the very knowledge of which man and his God are made consciously one. With the giving of the Name, the new initiate became himself a *pyramid*, within the chambers of whose soul numberless other human beings might also receive spiritual enlightenment.

In the King's Chamber was enacted the drama of the "second death." Here the candidate, after being crucified upon the cross of the solstices and the equinoxes, was buried in the great coffer. There is a profound mystery to the atmosphere and temperature of the King's Chamber: it is of a peculiar deathlike cold which cuts to the marrow of the bone. This room was a doorway between the material world and the transcendental spheres of Nature. While his body lay in the coffer, the soul of the neophyte soared as a human-headed hawk through the celestial realms, there to discover first hand the eternity of Life, Light, and Truth, as well as the illusion of Death, Darkness, and Sin. Thus in one sense the Great Pyramid may be likened to a gate through which the ancient priests permitted a few to pass toward the attainment of individual completion. It is also to be noted incidentally that if the coffer in the King's Chamber be struck, the sound emitted has no counterpart in any known musical scale. This tonal value may have formed part of that combination of circumstances which rendered the

King's Chamber an ideal setting for the conferment of the highest degree of the Mysteries.

The modern world knows little of these ancient rites. The scientist and the theologian alike gaze upon the sacred structure, wondering what fundamental urge inspired the herculean labor. If they would but think for a moment, they would realize that there is only one urge in the soul of man capable of supplying the required incentive--namely, the desire to know, to understand, and to exchange the narrowness of human mortality for the greater breadth and scope of divine enlightenment. So men say of the Great Pyramid that it is the most perfect building in the world, the source of weights and measures, the original Noah's Ark, the origin of languages, alphabets,. and scales of temperature and humidity. Few realize, however, that it is the gateway to the Eternal.

Though the modern world may know a million secrets, the ancient world knew one--and that one was greater than the million; for the *million* secrets breed death, disaster, sorrow, selfishness, lust, and avarice, but the *one* secret confers life, light, and truth. The time will come when the secret wisdom shall again be the dominating religious and philosophical urge of the world. The day is at hand when the doom of dogma shall be sounded. The great theological Tower of Babel, with its confusion of tongues, was built of bricks of mud and the mortar of slime. Out of the cold ashes of lifeless creeds, however, shall rise *phœnixlike* the ancient Mysteries. No other institution has so completely satisfied the religious aspirations of humanity, for since the destruction of the Mysteries there never has been a religious code to which Plato could have subscribed. The unfolding of man's spiritual nature is as much an exact science as astronomy, medicine or jurisprudence. To accomplish this end religions were primarily established; and out of religion have come science, philosophy, and logic as methods whereby this divine purpose might be realized.

The Dying God shall rise again! The secret room in the House of the Hidden Places shall be rediscovered. The Pyramid again shall stand as the ideal emblem of solidarity, inspiration, aspiration, resurrection, and regeneration. As the passing sands of time bury civilization upon civilization beneath their weight, the Pyramid shall remain as the Visible covenant between Eternal Wisdom and the world. The time may yet come when the chants of the illumined shall be heard once more in its ancient passageways and the Master of the Hidden House shall await in the Silent Place for the coming of that man who, casting aside the fallacies of dogma and tenet, seeks simply Truth and will be satisfied with neither substitute nor counterfeit.

www.ingramcontent.com/pod-product-compliance
Lightning Source LLC
Chambersburg PA
CBHW061317040426
42444CB00010B/2685